GW00402057

SURREY AERONAUTICS
AND AVIATION
1785 - 1985

Frontispiece: **Sir Alliott Verdon-Roe** returns to Brooklands in June 1954 and is pictured here standing by the memorial, which has just been unveiled, in the Paddock close to the site of his original workshops of 1908. *[Courtesy of Brooklands Museum]*

SURREY AERONAUTICS AND AVIATION 1785 - 1985

BY
SIR PETER G. MASEFIELD

[The following is the text of a paper presented to the Surrey Local History Council Symposium on "Road, Rail and Air"on Saturday, 16th. November, 1985 at the University of Surrey, Guildford. In view of its historical importance, it is given here in its entirety, un-edited.

Unless otherwise attributed the illustrations have been provided by Sir Peter Masefield himself. The quality of some of the illustrations is not up to modern standards, but they have been included for their great historic interest.]

Cover Illustration: **HP42 Hanno G - AAUD** over Croydon, July 1931.

Published by
PHILLIMORE
for
SURREY LOCAL HISTORY COUNCIL

Published by
PHILLIMORE & CO. LTD.
Shopwyke Manor Barn, Chichester, Sussex, England

for
SURREY LOCAL HISTORY COUNCIL
Guildford, Surrey

as extra volume number six of
Surrey History.

© Sir Peter G. Masefield 1993

ISBN 0 85033 891 3

SURREY AERONAUTICS AND AVIATION 1785 - 1985

May I say what a great pleasure it is to be with you at this meeting of the Surrey Local History Council and to have been invited to speak on the historic sites from which aeronautics (lighter-than-air) and aviation (heavier-than-air flying) have sprung in Surrey; specifically the sites which have been the launching pads - successively - of balloons, airships and, then, aeroplanes.

It is a history which extends now for more than 200 years and it embraces more than 40 different sites - from Hurst Park in 1785, to Gatwick and Dunsfold today. In the time and space available, I can do no more than touch on the highlights, starting with the 29th June, 1785, ever since when Surrey has been closely involved with British aeronautics and British aviation in peace and war. Today, Gatwick Airport, within the historic boundaries of Surrey - although officially now - and I think, unfortunately - translated into West Sussex, is the second busiest airport in the United Kingdom (after Heathrow) and it is, furthermore, in terms of passengers handled the World's fourth most important international airport - after Heathrow, J.F.K., New York, and Frankfurt. On the military side, Dunsfold, near Guildford, is today one of the most important of the experimental and production flight centres of British Aerospace, the home of the Harrier VTOL development. In all, over the years, there have been 45 different geographical sites of aeronautical activity in Surrey. Twelve of them were sites from which balloons were flown in the early days of manned ascents. They were succeeded by 20 aerodromes, airports or landing strips for fixed-wing aircraft. And there are now eleven licensed helicopter pads in Surrey.

Chronologically, those 45 sites of aeronautical activities in Surrey can be divided into eight, distinct, phases:

The first - ballooning; from 1785 to 1920. This period of 135 years of flight in lighter-than-air craft (balloons and airships) saw flights made from twelve different sites in Surrey; notably the grounds of the Crystal Palace in Upper Norwood and from the Ranelagh Club grounds at Barn Elms.

The second - the first aerodromes; from 1907 to 1914 covered the early days of fixed-wing, heavier-than-air craft up to the outbreak of war in 1914. During those pioneering years of mechanical flight, there were five early aerodromes in Surrey; the most important of them in the centre of the Brooklands Motor Race Track at Weybridge. Brooklands remained active in aviation for more than 60 years.

The Third Phase was that of the First World War from 1914 to 1918. Again, Brooklands was much the most significant of the five aerodromes active in Surrey during those five years which saw, also, the beginnings of flying on what was later to become part of Croydon Airport.

Fourth was the period of the early peace-time development of British aviation in the eleven years between 1919 and 1930. During that decade there were five active sites in Surrey; notably still Brooklands and the airport which was steadily becoming the most important centre of international air transport of those days - "The London Terminal Airport" at Croydon.

The Fifth Phase - from 1931 to 1939 - saw the blossoming of both air transport and the "Golden Age of Private Flying" which grew up around the de Havilland Moths, the Miles Hawks and the Percival Gulls. There were, during those nine years, eight busy aerodromes in Surrey, Croydon Airport in the lead, with Gatwick growing up to the South, Brooklands still busy with aircraft manufacture and club flying, Redhill developing and Kenley an important base for the Air Defence of Great Britain.

The Sixth Phase - covered the Second World War in the six years between 1939 and 1945. Twelve aerodromes were in the thick of it in Surrey - Brooklands, the centre of fighter and bomber production and development by Hawker and Vickers Armstrongs Limited; with Royal Air Force Fighter Stations at Kenley, Croydon, Gatwick, Redhill, Hurst Park, Egham, Dunsfold and Horne - all active in the Battle of Britain with Wisley reinforcing Brooklands as Vickers Armstrongs' base for development and production flying.

The Seventh Phase covered the first 20 years of the post-war transition from war to an uneasy peace. The eight remaining sites in Surrey were reduced to only four by the end of this period, when first Croydon, and then Kenley, historic Brooklands and, finally, Wisley, were all run down and ceased to contribute to the aviation scene.

And now - **The Eighth Phase** - the past 20 years from 1965 to 1985, finds Surrey reduced to five centres for fixed-wing flying - with Gatwick Airport still growing fast, with Dunsfold a centre for military and naval aircraft development, and Redhill and Fairoaks available for general aviation. In addition, there are now ten, licensed, helicopter pads.

Out of all the 45 aerodromes, balloon sites and helicopter pads which have existed in Surrey during the past 200 years, five stand out pre-eminently. In order of seniority they have been:-

1. **Brooklands** at Weybridge - between 1909 and 1975;

2. **Kenley Aerodrome** at Upper Warlingham - between 1917 and 1965;

3. **Croydon Airport** off Purley Way - from 1920 to 1959;

4. **Gatwick Airport** near Horley - from 1930 onwards; and

5. **Dunsfold Airfield** near Cranleigh - from 1943 onwards.

And, of these five, Brooklands remains the most historic and Gatwick the most significant, and, I suspect, likely to be the most enduring.

Surrey's aerodromes have - thus - had a distinguished record through two World Wars and into the jet age of civil Jumbos and advanced military Vertical-Take-Off fighters - the Harrier. They have been, and they remain, of major national importance - a contribution to both national defence and to employment and prosperity. Surrey's contribution to aeronautics and, through it, to our national defence and to peace-time prosperity, has, thus, been in the forefront of technological progress throughout the years. I wish that I could record that bodies, such as the Surrey County Council (and Surrey's Members of Parliament) in general, had showed more enthusiasm towards aviation than they have done in recent years - or do at present. Looked at, objectively, one has to say that Aviation, and employment in the high technology of aeronautics, has developed in Surrey 'in spite of' rather than 'thanks to' official attitudes since the War. Dedication and enthusiasm, combined with hard work and a refusal to be discouraged, has, fortunately, been a hall-mark of the British aeronautical community in Surrey since the early days - as elsewhere. As a result, Surrey has - now for 200 years - been in the forefront of progress at those 45 geographical sites for both lighter-than-air and heavier-than-air craft.

Ballooning

Going back to the beginnings, it all 'took off' just eighteen months after the world's first manned balloon-ascent on 21st. November, 1783, made by Pilatre de Rozier and the Marquis d'Arlandes, from the Chateau la Meutte in the Bois de Boulogne, Paris. That first manned ascent lasted for 25 minutes and covered a distance of about 5 miles, down wind, over Paris, in their hot-air Montgolfier balloon, fuelled by burning straw.

In Surrey, on 1st. May, 1785, James Sadler - the first English aeronaut - ascended in a hydrogen balloon from Hurst Park, Molesey, beside the River Thames - then known as Moulsey Hurst. Sadler was accompanied by William Windham, Member of Parliament for Norwich and later Minister of War and for the Colonies in Grenville's administration. Ascending from Hurst Park, they passed over Southwark, Blackheath and Dartford and, wisely, valved gas to come down on the Isle of Grain near the confluence of the River Thames and the Medway, so as to avoid being blown out to sea. That was the third flight by Sadler, the first from Surrey soil and the tenth flight to have been made in the British Isles.

In fact, the first balloon journey in England had taken place some eight months before - made by the Italian, Vincent Lunardi, who had ascended from the grounds of the Honourable Artillery Company at Moorfields in the City of London, on 15th. September, 1784.

During the next 140 years, eleven other sites were used in Surrey as the bases of balloon flying. Surrey's second link with the Balloon Era came eight weeks after Sadler's flight from Hurst Park, when - on 29th. June, 1785 - Lunardi, in order to promote publicity and so keep himself financially in the public eye, invited an attractive, but otherwise undistinguished, English actress, Mrs. Letysia Sage, to fly with him on his projected third ascent, accompanied, this time, by his (and, I suspect, her) financial backer, Colonel George Biggin, and by another lady and a Colonel Hastings. That comprised an ambitious payload of five in all. The site for the ascent was the so-called 'Garden of Amusement' at St. George's Fields, Southwark, surrounding the, so-called, Royal Circle (now St. George's Circus) where Blackfriars Road meets Westminster Bridge Road and Lambeth Road. For the ascent, the thirteenth in Britain, Lunardi provided his new hydrogen balloon, painted with the Union Jack, and prepared to take off before a large crowd. The five prospective aeronauts piled into the basket, but their weight proved too much for the lifting capacity of the balloon. All except Mrs. Sage and Colonel Biggin then scrambled out and - relieved of their weight - the balloon shot up while Mrs. Sage, the first lady aeronaut in England, kissed her hands to everyone below as they sailed over Westminster Bridge, St. James's and Piccadilly, to come down, two hours later, on Harrow Common before a delighted group of boys from Harrow School.

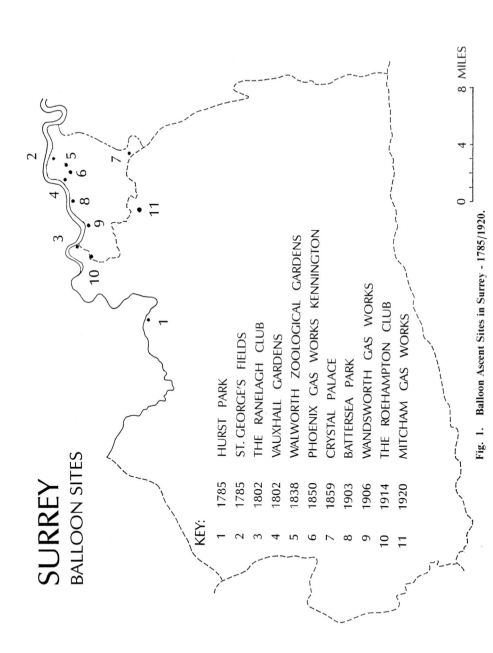

SURREY
BALLOON SITES

KEY:

1	1785	HURST PARK
2	1785	ST. GEORGE'S FIELDS
3	1802	THE RANELAGH CLUB
4	1802	VAUXHALL GARDENS
5	1838	WALWORTH ZOOLOGICAL GARDENS
6	1850	PHOENIX GAS WORKS KENNINGTON
7	1859	CRYSTAL PALACE
8	1903	BATTERSEA PARK
9	1906	WANDSWORTH GAS WORKS
10	1914	THE ROEHAMPTON CLUB
11	1920	MITCHAM GAS WORKS

Fig. 1. Balloon Ascent Sites in Surrey - 1785/1920.

0   4   8 MILES

4

A second ascent was made from the same St. George's Fields two months later on 31st. August, 1785. This time the aeronaut was Stuart Arnold, who ran the Garden of Amusement, with his twelve-year-old son, George. On a steady northerly wind, Arnold announced that his flight would be the first air journey from London to Paris. Unfortunately, the basket hit the railings around the St. George's Rotunda on take-off. It tipped out Stuart Arnold, leaving young George alone on board - to descend a few minutes later in the Thames at Rotherhithe, fortunately to be rescued, little the worse for a ducking.

For those first few years, as a new phenomenon, ballooning attracted continued interest up and down the country. Then, after 1786, that interest declined until there was a brief resurgence at the beginning of the 19th. century. In London, on the Surrey shore of the River Thames, this resurgence centred on another fashionable site, the Vauxhall Gardens in South Lambeth - earlier called Spring Gardens - the Disneyland of its day. The site of Vauxhall Gardens is now covered by St. Peter's Church, Vauxhall, and its adjacent streets between St. Oswald's Place, Vauxhall Street and Kennington Lane near the Kennington Oval. So extensive were these Gardens that it was stated at the time that "the windings and turnings in the wildernesses are so intricate that the most experienced mothers often lose themselves in looking for their daughters." The first ascent from the Vauxhall Gardens was by the Frenchman, A.J. Garnerin on 3rd. August, 1802.

By 1829, there had been, in all, 471 balloon aeronauts, of whom, 313 were British, 104 French, 18 Italian, 17 German, and five Turkish. The most experienced was Charles Green who with his brothers, sons and nephews, made 535 ascents. In spite of the unpredictable nature of the voyages down-wind, of the 471 balloonists, there had been only nine fatalities.

Yet another site in Surrey for balloon ascents was inaugurated on 24th. May, 1838, when, to celebrate Queen Victoria's birthday, J.W. Hoare attempted, unsuccessfully, to ascend in his 'Great Montgolfier' hot air balloon from a lake in the middle of the Surrey Zoological Gardens at Walworth. Between July, 1821, and September, 1852, the English aeronaut, Charles Green, made 500 balloon ascents, most of them from the Vauxhall Gardens, including a flight from Vauxhall to Elbern, Weilburg, in Nassau, Germany, a distance of 480 miles, between 7th. and 8th. November, 1836. A little earlier than this, in August, 1823, a Mr. and Mrs. George Graham made an adventurous landfall on Reigate Hill, flying from Paddington, when a grapnel on the end of a trailing rope from their balloon became entangled in the iron bridge on Reigate Hill and unceremoniously tipped out the Grahams into the bushes which surrounded the cutting there.

A new site, the Crystal Palace, just in Surrey at Upper Norwood, came into the picture for the first time when Henry Coxwell and James Glaisher ascended there in 1859, shortly after the Crystal Palace, originally in Hyde Park, had been re-erected on the Surrey/Kent borders near Sydenham. Thereafter, the grounds of the Crystal Palace became a favourite site for balloon inflation and ascents. By 1866, however, there was a growing interest in the possibilities of mechanical flight, enhanced by the foundation of the Aeronautical Society of Great Britain in January, 1866, and its holding at the Crystal Palace, on 25th. June, 1868, of the first Aeronautical Exhibition.

Fig. 2. Mr. Stanley Spencer's Air Ship, Starting on his Voyage from Crystal Palace to St. Paul's, 23rd. October, 1903. *(Courtesy of John Gent.)*

Fig. 3. Aero Club Balloons at Ranelagh, 1907.

Ten years later, in 1878, the first experimental British Military Balloon Section was formed at Woolwich, followed, in 1890, by a Balloon Section of the Royal Engineers at Aldershot. Then came, from 1895 to 1914, what one might call the Golden Age of balloon flying for sport, greatly encouraged by the founding, on 4th. September, 1901, of the Aero Club of the United Kingdom (later, the Royal Aero Club) when Frank Hedges Butler (a well known wine merchant of those days) with his daughter, Vera, and the Honourable Charles Rolls (of Rolls-Royce fame) ascended with the balloonist, Stanley Spencer, from the Crystal Palace and came down with the Articles of Association of the future Royal Aero Club all mapped out.

Then, on 31st. May, 1902, the first Balloon Meeting, organised by the Aero Club of Great Britain, was held at the polo ground of the Ranelagh Club at Barn Elms, just West of Barnes Common, where an inaugural race was won by Frank Hedges Butler with a flight from Ranelagh to Ongar in Essex. The Ranelagh Club became the base for aero club ballooning for the next five years until January, 1908, when it moved to the Hurlingham Club on the north bank of the Thames at Fulham. By the start of the new century, powered airships were beginning to appear and there took place the first cross-country flight by an airship in Britain, from the Crystal Palace to Eastcote in Middlesex on 22nd. September, 1902, and then, on 5th. October, 1907, the British Army airship, 'Nulli Secundus', flew from Aldershot to the Crystal Palace. It was followed, on 18th. November, 1908, by a balloon distance record from the Crystal Palace to Mateki Derevni in the province of New Alexandrovsk, in Russia, 1,117 miles in 36 hours - a remarkable flight made by A.E. Gaudron, Captain E.A. Maitland and Major C.C. Turner, in a large balloon of 108,000 cubic feet, appropriately named the 'Mammoth'. Airships were by now coming into the picture and a third flight to the Crystal Palace grounds was made, this time by the 'Willows Airship No. Two', flying from Cardiff on 6th. and 7th. August, 1910, and covering 140 miles in ten hours.

Although, by now, heavier-than-air craft were beginning to appear, the sport of free-balloon flying, specially on the part of the Royal Aero Club, was enjoying a revival of popularity. It was made the easier by the fact that coal gas was widely available and so ascents were increasingly made from the vicinity of gas-works; in May, 1850, from the Phoenix Gas-works adjoining Kennington Oval, from 1903 from the Battersea Gas-works on the Surrey side of Chelsea Bridge and from the Wandsworth Gas-works from which, on 27th. November, 1906, a notable flight was made to Vevey in Switzerland in 16 hours. A link between ballooning and the start of mechanical flight in heavier-than-air craft was forged by the Short Brothers - Horace, Eustace and Oswald - who, in 1903, rented two arches under the London, Brighton and South Coast Railway at Battersea Park, next to the Battersea Gas-works, for the building and inflation of balloons. Coal gas had substantially less lifting capacity than hydrogen but it was much easier to obtain and very much cheaper. The Short Brothers supplied balloons to the Royal Aero Club and to the Royal Navy, which had set up a Balloon Training Centre at Roehampton.

The Wright Brothers came to Battersea on 3rd May, 1908, met the Short Brothers and entered into an agreement whereby the Short Brothers would build six Wright Flyers under the arches at Battersea alongside their balloon activities. So, for a time, ballooning and aircraft construction went along side by side, Oswald Short, in particular, flying balloons from Battersea Park. Before we leave the subject of balloons over Surrey, I must quote from an enthusiastic account written by Major C.C. Turner in 1910. He wrote:-

"I am alone in a very small balloon over Surrey on the last day of a beautiful May. So light is the wind that on that little voyage three hours and a half were taken to travel 16 miles from Roehampton to Betchworth. There is scarcely a cloud in the sky. The sun is hot and the balloon, being inflated with hydrogen, is very lively. Hydrogen is much more sensitive to heat and cold than coal gas and the basket is quite tiny. Two men in it would be a crowd."

"I am alone and as the hours pass the loneliness becomes rather oppressive. This is quite different from aeroplaning for there is little to occupy the attention and scarcely anything to do with the hands. Plenty of time to look around and down."

"Very slowly, I approach a big wood. It would better express the situation were I to say that very slowly the big wood comes nearer to the balloon for there is no sense of movement and the earth below seems to be moving slowly past the stationary balloon."

"1,500 feet up and almost absolute silence, broken occasionally by the barking of a dog, heard very faintly, or by a voice hailing the balloon. Then, quite suddenly, I am aware of something new. My attention is arrested by a new sound - surely the most wonderful and the sweetest sound heard by mortal ears. It is the combined singing of thousands of birds of half the kinds which make the English Spring so lovely. I do not hear one above the others; all are blended together in a wonderful harmony, without change of pitch or tone, yet never wearying the ear. By very close attention, I seem to be able, at times, to pick out an individual song. No doubt at all there are wrens and chaffinches and blackbirds and thrushes, hedge-sparrows, warblers, greenfinches and bullfinches and a score of others by the hundred. And their singing comes up to me from the ten-acre wood in one sweet volume of heavenly music."

"The balloon steadily mounts to 7,000 feet, for the sun is very hot. Awakening, as it seems, from a beautiful dream, I begin to think of a place to land. There are the Southern slopes of the Surrey Hills. I pick out Reigate, Betchworth, Dorking and, far away to the South, I see the South Downs and the gleam of the Channel. But with the end of my ballast approaching, I must prepare to land. My course will take me right over Betchworth and there is a railway station which will save me a lot of trouble. I valve the gas and the balloon promptly begins to fall."

"Rather a heavy landing and I am down in the basket, huddled up by the fall. Then it bounces and comes down again almost on the same spot. The people of the village assemble and offer help."

"Elsewhere, on another occasion, there is another beautiful sound only the balloonist hears. It is the music of a million waves, unsullied by the rolling of breaking waves on sand or shingle or against the side of a ship. This is unique to the balloonist."

And that epitomises, I think, the especial delights of free-ballooning. But so much for that early era which came, more or less, to an end with the start of the First World War, although there were some desultory balloon ascents after the War up till about 1920. And now, as we know, the hot-air balloon, made buoyant by calor-gas, is returning to the skies, though limited by the problems of air traffic control.

Powered-controlled Flight - 'The Aeroplane Era'

Heavier-than-air flying of powered aircraft in Surrey goes back, now, 79 years to September, 1907, when the Brooklands Automobile Racing Club offered a prize of £ 2,500 to the first man who would fly around the track before the end of that year. Alliot Verdon-Roe (who had won a prize at the Crystal Palace for a model aeroplane in 1906) went to Brooklands with a scaled-up, man-carrying version of his model aeroplane. He could, however, achieve no more than short hops in this first Avro biplane. But, a year later on 8th. June, 1908, he managed to become airborne and covered about 100 feet along the Brooklands Finishing Straight. It was not recognised as a powered and controlled flight but it was the first time that an Englishman had left the ground under his own power. The first sustained aeroplane flight in Great Britain was achieved on 16th. October, 1908, at Laffan's Plain, South Farnborough, Hampshire, when Samuel Cody flew 1,390 feet in a biplane of his own design and construction.

Fig. 4.   A.V.Roe and the Roe I Biplane in its shed at Brooklands c.1908. *[Courtesy of Brooklands Museum]*

One other site of sustained, powered, flight in heavier-than-air craft came into every-day use ahead of Brooklands. It was Shellbeach, at Leysdown, on the Isle of Sheppey, where on 30th. April, 1909, J.T.C. Moore-Brabazon (later to be Lord Brabazon of Tara and President of the Royal Aero Club) made three short flights in a somewhat rickety Voisin biplane, incongruously named "Bird of Passage". They were the first flights of a British born Briton in Britain. Mussel Manor at Shellbeach became the Royal Aero Club's headquarters for powered flight; the Short Brothers established an assembly works in a hangar there in

April, 1909, and on Tuesday, 4th. May, the Wright Brothers visited it to inspect the assembly of Wright biplanes built by Shorts under licence. Moore-Brabazon made the first circular mile flight by an Englishman at Leysdown on 30th. October, 1909, flying a British built Short-Wright aeroplane, thereby winning the *Daily Mail* prize of £ 1,000. Leysdown remained an active aerodrome, eventually a Royal Air Force Station, as an emergency landing ground under the aegis of R.A.F. Eastchurch until after the Second World War.

Surrey came into the picture for powered flight just one year after Cody's first flight in Britain on Laffan's Plain. On 29th. October, 1909, the French pioneer airman, Louis Paulhan (later to win the London (Hendon) to Manchester Air Race) inaugurated the interior of the Motor Race Track at Brooklands, near Weybridge, as an aerodrome with what was billed as "Three Days of Exhibition Flying at the Weybridge Bowl." Large crowds came to Brooklands to watch the first public demonstration of flying in England by a heavier-than-air machine. It was a Henry Farman biplane, built in France but designed by one of the two English Farman brothers living there. After heavy October rains which resulted in heavy floods in the centre of the Race Track, Paulhan made 15 flights on the Friday, Saturday and Monday of 29th. October to 1st. November, 1909 - the Sabbath Day being rigorously observed with no flying permitted. Paulhan's flight on 1st. November, 1909, was the longest performed in England up to that time. It was of two hours 49 minutes 29 seconds duration and it won a 50 guinea trophy for the longest non-stop distance flown in Great Britain - 96 miles.

Having completed his demonstrations at Brooklands and having thereby established a Surrey aerodrome, Paulhan took his Farman bi-plane to the nearby Sandown Park Racecourse at Esher. He flew there first on Friday, 5th. November, 1909, watched by Lord Roberts and Lord Charles Berisford on behalf of the War Office and the Admiralty. Next day, 6th. November, he set up a new British record for flying a circular mile in two minutes one second - at almost 30 miles an hour. Later that day, in a flight of 16 minutes at Sandown Park, he set up a new World's height record of 977 feet - measured so precisely by the Royal Engineers through the use of a theodolite. Bad weather then curtailed flying in England for the rest of 1909.

So Paulhan's flying at Brooklands and at Sandown Park in the Autumn of that year were the first public demonstrations of controlled flight in Britain. Very short - and only semi-controlled, or even uncontrolled - hops had been made in England, and in Surrey, ahead of that time. The very first appears to have been by Horatio Phillips with his unmanned 'multiplane' at Streatham Common in June of 1907 and then, as already mentioned, on 8th. June, 1908, by A.V. Roe in his 24-horse-power Avro No. 1 bi-plane on the Finishing Straight at Brooklands. Neither of these efforts were recognised as genuine flights. The first recognised flight at Brooklands by an Englishman was in December, 1909, when J.V. Neale achieved a straight flight of a few hundred feet at a height of about 20 feet in a Bleriot-replica monoplane. Later, the Neale Pup - a Bleriot-type monoplane - was the first aeroplane to be designed and flown in Surrey and at Brooklands.

The year 1909 had, thus, seen the beginnings of the establishment of aeroplane flying in Britain - at Farnborough, at Leysdown, at Brooklands and at Eastchurch. Farnborough was then, and remained, a base for military aeronautics under the War Office, then under the Air Ministry and - more recently - under Ministry of Defence control. Leysdown and Eastchurch were originated by the Royal Aero Club. Leysdown was taken over by the Royal Flying Corps and then by the Royal Air Force while Eastchurch became the first base of Naval Aviation, and then of the Royal Naval Air Service before it was amalgamated with the Royal Flying Corps to form the Royal Air Force on 1st. April, 1918. By contrast, Brooklands was always the home of private enterprise in aviation; the chief centre of flying schools and of the pioneering British aircraft constructors.

Early Aerodromes

In those first, pioneering, days of powered flight in heavier-than-air machines, nine aerodromes in Britain became the established centres of flying and of aeronautical enthusiasm generally. These nine were backed up by a substantial number of other sites from which flights were made in the early days although none of them survived as recognised aerodromes into the future. The initial nine sites which remained active throughout the early days of British aviation were - in chronological order -

1. LAFFAN'S PLAIN, South Farnborough, Hampshire.
   (S.F. Cody)   16th. OCTOBER 1908.

2. SHELLBEACH, Leysdown, Isle of Sheppey, Kent.
   (J.C.T. Moore-Brabazon)   30th. APRIL 1909.

3. BROOKLANDS, Byfleet, Surrey.
   (Louis Paulhan)   29th. OCTOBER 1909.

4. EASTCHURCH, Isle of Sheppey, Kent.
   (Hon. Charles Rolls)   20th. NOVEMBER 1909.

5. LARKHILL (Stonehenge), Amesbury, Salisbury Plain, Wiltshire.
   (B. Woodrow)   JANUARY 1910.

6. HENDON, Colindale, Middlesex.
   (Louis Paulhan)   27th. APRIL 1910.

7. BEALIEU, Brockenhurst, Hampshire.
   (A. Drexel)   MAY, 1910.

8. NEW SALTS FARM, Shoreham, Sussex.
   (H.H. Pifford)   10th. JULY 1910.

9. FILTON, Bristol.
   (M. Edmond)   AUGUST 1910.

It is a somewhat sad commentary that of these nine historic sites of British aviation, only Farnborough in Hampshire, Shoreham in Sussex and Filton, Bristol, remain as active aerodromes today. As a matter of record, the additional sites at which there were intermittent flights during the first few years of British aviation, included - in alphabetical order - Barking, Blackpool, Blair Atholl, Bournemouth, Camber Sands, Crystal Palace, Dagenham, Doncaster, Dunhill Park (Wolverhampton), Folkestone, Hounslow Heath, Huntingdon, Lanark, Lea Marshes, Littlehampton, Newbury, Park Royal, Rye, Saltburn, Wembley Park and Wormwood Scrubs.

Fig. 5.   Mr. Grahame White, flying from Crystal Palace in July 1910. The message on the postcard mentions his 'Burbery' windproof flying suit. *[courtesy of John Gent]*

12

Only one of those original aerodromes was, thus, in Surrey but Brooklands made up for that by the intensity and the breadth of its involvement in aviation in those early years. Indeed, over the whole field of early British aviation up to the start of the First World War, some three-quarters of the serious work on the development of aircraft and of the training of pilots took place at Brooklands where Sopwith, Avro, Howard Wright, Martin and Handasyde, Howard Flanders and Vickers Limited all used Brooklands as their major development centres. On the other hand, public entertainment was a minor feature of Brooklands in those days because that would interfere with the major work of practical aeronautics. By contrast, Hendon concentrated on entertainment for the public with pylon racing, passenger flights, night flying and displays of aerobatics with attendances of more than 20,000 people at the regular weekend meetings there. Of all the centres of British aviation between 1909 and 1914 - those first Golden Years of enterprise, enthusiasm and activity in British aviation - Brooklands, under Lindsay Lloyd, was right in the forefront - its social life and ardent discussion-centre grouped around the 'Blue Bird' cafe, run by Mr. and Mrs. Eardley Billing in the original Paulhan Sheds which had been vacated by Helmuth Martin and George Handasyde by Easter, 1910, when they moved into new, larger, hangars.

The pioneering inhabitants of the Brooklands village at this time included Alliot Verdon-Roe with his first triplanes flown by Howard Pixton, Claude Grahame White with his Farman biplanes, Noel Pemberton Billing, E.C. Gordon England and Herbert Wood of Vickers. The first flying school at Brooklands was opened in 1910 jointly by Gustav Blondeau and Mrs. Maurice Hewlett - who taught her son to fly there, the first naval officer to be taught by his mother. Next came the Bristol School, organised by Harry Delacombe - and then, on 4th. November, 1910, Tom Sopwith took off successfully for the first time without any dual instruction, at Brooklands, flying a Howard Wright biplane. Seventeen days later, he gained his Royal Aero Club Certificate - No. 31 - and less than a month after that, won the £ 4,000 Baron de Forest prize for the longest non-stop flight from England to the Continent of Europe when, on 18th. December, 1910, he flew his Howard Wright biplane a distance of 177 miles in three hours 40 minutes to Beaumont in Belgium. So, flying at Brooklands progressed with steadily increasing activity. On 25th. September, 1913, there was another 'milestone' when it was the scene of the first looping of the loop in Britain. This was by the Frenchman, Louis Pègout, in a Bleriot monoplane, in front of the biggest crowd seen at any aerodrome in Britain up to that time.

Brooklands became famous for its aerodrome, for its race track and for one other prominent feature - its sewage farm - which seemed to have a magnetic attraction as a soft landing place for some of the early aviators, who suffered from the chronic engine troubles of the day. Indeed, the wife of the owner of Brooklands, Dame Ethel Locke-King, on her first flight in 1911, suffered engine failure on take-off, just cleared the sewage farm and finished up in the River Wey, from which she was fished out, wet but uninjured.

So it was that in those early days of British aviation - up to August, 1914 - Brooklands, with Farnborough, Leysdown, Salisbury Plain, Eastchurch and Hendon were the six aerodromes which had the greatest influence on the future of British aviation. Up to the outbreak of War on 4th. August, 1914, the ten flying schools at Brooklands had trained a total of 318 pilots, of whom 182 had

Fig. 6. T.O.M. Sopwith at Brooklands, *c.*1910. *[Courtesy of Brooklands Museum]*

Fig. 7. Tuning-up for Flight at Brooklands, from a postcard sent on 20th. July, 1911. *[Courtesy of John Gent]*

Fig. 8. **Flight Ticket Office, Brooklands** *c.*1911. *[Courtesy of Brooklands Museum].*

gained their Royal Aero Club Certificates at the Bristol School there, together with 77 at the Vickers School. Those totals compared with the 213 pilots trained in the same period at Hendon and with 153 trained by the Royal Flying Corps Schools at Upavon and Netheravon, with 17 Naval pilots trained at Eastchurch.

By the start of the First World War, therefore, six sites in Surrey had been the scenes of heavier-than-air flying, starting with early model experiments at the Crystal Palace in June of 1875, going on through Horatio Phillips' hops with his multi-plane at Streatham Common in May of 1907, A.V. Roe at Brooklands in June of 1908 and the first real flights in Surrey by Paulhan at Brooklands in October, 1909, and at Sandown Park in November, 1909, followed by Cyril Ridley's gliding flights at Sandown Park in 1910 and by the Passat ornithopter at Wimbledon Common in 1912 - where it flew for 150 yards before being damaged beyond repair by hitting a tree. The Great War of 1914-18 was to bring on to the aviation scene three new sites in Surrey, with Brooklands remaining by far the most important.

LEARN TO FLY

. . . at the . . .

VICKERS

FLYING SCHOOL

BROOKLANDS.

Thoroughly graded tuition from slow Biplane to fast Monoplane

Instructing a Pupil. Note Instructor sitting behind Pupil.

Special Terms to Naval and Military Officers.

VICKERS, Limited,

Aviation Department,

VICKERS HOUSE, BROADWAY,
LONDON, S.W.

Fig. 9. Vickers Flying School, Brooklands, from an advertisement in *The Aeroplane* of 1st. January 1914.

The Great War 1914-18

Just as Brooklands had been one of the original cradles of British heavier-than-air flying, so Brooklands continued to be a centre of major aeronautical activity right through the First World War - the 'Great War' of 1914-18. But, contrary to a widely held view, although the two wars (1914-18 and 1939-45) pushed forward the development of aircraft and aero-engines (because of the rate of expenditure of money and effort in improving the breed), nevertheless both the wars had a devastating effect upon the smooth progress of aviation as an everyday pursuit. In particular, Brooklands was deflected from its role as a home of flying training and of sound economic manufacture for a period of more than ten years from 1914. During the First World War, its role changed from that of primarily civil flying - the flying schools, civil aircraft manufacture in small numbers and air races and other competitions - to that of a major centre of aircraft assembly and of test flying. After the Second World War, Brooklands had been transformed from a popular motor race track and thriving school of flying to a desert of broken concrete dominated by massive production lines, not appropriate to peace-time requirements.

Brooklands was taken over by the War Office on 5th. August, 1914, and the motor race-track was closed to the public. No. 8 Squadron, Royal Flying Corps, was formed at Brooklands on 1st. January, 1915, and worked up there before flying to France on 15th. April, equipped with B.E.2C aircraft. Meanwhile, increasing numbers of Sopwith aircraft, built at Kingston, were assembled and test flown at Brooklands, together with the Martinsydes and Avro 504s and, from August, 1915, the first of a long range of Vickers aircraft, including, initially the 'Gunbus'. Eventually, Vickers built more than 1,650 S.E.5A's at Brooklands under contract to the Royal Aircraft Factory at Farnborough. In all, during the War, four Brooklands-based companies built some 21,757 aircraft, though not all of them at Brooklands. They included more than 11,000 Sopwith aircraft, more than 8,000 Avros, some 240 Vickers aircraft and 300 Martinsydes.

But Brooklands was not alone in Surrey as a centre of War-time aeronautical activity, although it was by far the most important. From December, 1915, an aerodrome was established by the Royal Flying Corps at Beddington, south of Stafford Road and west of Plough Lane and two miles south west of Croydon. This Beddington/Wallington aerodrome was instituted as part of the air defence of London and B.E.2C aircraft from there ascended to attack raiding Zeppelins on the nights of January 31st., March 31st. and 2nd. April, 1916, and against aeroplanes which raided London during daylight on 31st. June and 7th. July 1917. During this period, a training squadron was also stationed at Beddington, at first, No. 17 (Reserve) Training Squadron, Royal Flying Corps, and from 1917, No. 40 Training Squadron, R.F.C., and in 1918 No. 29 Training Squadron, on which His Royal Highness The Duke of York (Prince Albert) and later King George VI, obtained his Wings on an Avro 504 in 1919. During 1918, the Number One National Aircraft Factory was built on an adjoining site - Waddon Aerodrome - to the East of Plough Lane and adjoining Coldharbour Lane - now Purley Way. Complete D.H.9 aircraft were delivered from this Factory 24 weeks after the first turf had been cut on the site. The Waddon Aerodrome, opposite the new buildings, provided the test aerodrome for the National Factory in 1918. All this was the start of Croydon Airport from 1920. In the process of making these two aerodromes, eventually combined into one,

17

the lands of two farms and the track of an old Roman road were all incorporated into the eventual airport. New Barn Farm, from which a track ran east to Coldharbour Lane, was taken up within the Waddon Aerodrome. To the south, Cross Shaws Farm was, likewise, incorporated and on the west side of Plough Lane, Furze Edge Shaw Farm and Beggar's Bush Farm were both included.

Fig. 10. Aerial Lighthouse at Waddon Air Station *[Courtesy of John Gent.]*

In March, 1915, the War Office added Wimbledon Common to its list of auxiliary flying fields and night emergency landing grounds in the London area and B.E.2C aircraft, with night-trained pilots from reserve aeroplane squadrons, were based there from November, 1915. A B.E.2C (No. 2107) flown by Lieutenant H. Tomlinson crashed on take-off from Wimbledon Common in the dark on the night of 31st. January, 1916, when attempting to intercept a Zeppelin raid. Another aerodrome whlch was to become a permanent Royal Air Force station was brought into service in March of 1917. It was situated on the high ground of Kenley Common above Upper Warlingham and it was established, first of all, as Number Seven Aircraft Acceptance Park, Royal Flying Corps, and used, also, for the air defence of London with F.E.8 and R.E.8 aircraft - somewhat ineffective as interceptor fighters. Kenley went on to become a Royal Air Force fighter station from 1918 until 1965. Yet another air defence station of the Royal Flying Corps, with a brief service life, was instituted at Newchapel, 3 miles north west of East Grinstead, together with a return to the balloon site - and racecourse - at Hurst Park. During the First World War, therefore, Surrey had six active aerodromes - Beddington, Brooklands, Hurst Park, Kenley, Newchapel, Waddon and Wimbledon Common - of which Brooklands was, and remained, by far the most significant.

Early Peace-time Development

With the Armistice, on 11th. November, 1918, only Brooklands, Kenley and the Beddington/Waddon combination remained active - and they on a greatly reduced basis. Indeed, aviation in Britain was in such doldrums that the great Sopwith Aviation Company at Kingston and Weybridge decided, perforce, to go into voluntary liquidation on 10th. September, 1920 - to be succeeded in November of that year by the new, small, H.G. Hawker Engineering Company -

named for Harry Hawker, Sopwith's Chief Test Pilot and collaborator on aircraft design. Sadly, Harry Hawker was killed at the age of 30 on 12th. July, 1921, when flying a Sopwith/Hawker Goshawk in preparation for the Aerial Derby Air Race round London. Meanwhile, Vickers (Aviation) Limited had concentrated its aviation activities at Brooklands and, by 1924, was turning out Vimy Commercial transport aircraft for both home and overseas airlines, Vernon transports for the Royal Air Force and Viking single-engine amphibians - all under the design leadership of Rex Pearson.

Meanwhile, 16 miles away, off Coldharbour Lane, between Croydon and Purley, the two, former, military aerodromes of Waddon and Beddington had been combined - by means of an aircraft level crossing over Plough Lane between the two - to form, from Sunday, 28th. March, 1920, "The Official Air Terminus for London", soon to be known as Croydon Airport. The story of Croydon Airport, for some nineteen years the World's most important international centre of air transport services, forms a chapter of aviation history all to itself. Here I must be brief. The part of the aerodrome used at first for commercial air services was that east of Plough Lane, adjoining the National Aircraft Factory, now taken over by Handley Page Limited from the Ministry of Munitions, to form the Aircraft Disposal Company, from which, for three years from April, 1920, the Department of Civil Aviation at the Air Ministry leased the use of Croydon Aerodrome. The hangars for the commercial aircraft were, however, on the west side of Plough Lane, to which they taxied over the level crossing. The Royal Flying Corps huts on Plough Lane served as the Terminal Buildings from the end of March, 1920, until 30th. January, 1928, when the move took place to the new, 'custom-built' airport buildings on Purley Way - officially opened on 2nd. May, 1928, by Lady Maude Hoare, wife of the Secretary of State for Air. Thereafter, Plough Lane was closed and grassed over while the original R.F.C. buildings on its side were demolished and replaced by the Croydon Passenger Terminal, the Airport Hotel and the Imperial Airways hangars, all of which still stand today - we hope, to be preserved for posterity, by the Croydon Airport Society in association with Guardian Royal Assurance Company and the Science Museum.

The first commercial flight out of Croydon was flown on 22nd. March, 1920, in a D.H.9 piloted by Captain Bayliss, leaving Croydon at 13.05 hours and arriving at Le Bourget, Paris, two hours and 15 minutes later. In its heyday, the dimensions of Croydon as an aerodrome were 1,150 yards square with a slight slope towards the north. In all its 33 years of active life in air transport and other civil aviation activities, Croydon Airport handled a total of some 1.9 million passengers, flying in some 655,000 aircraft movements at an average, therefore, of not quite three passengers on each aircraft. The beginnings of Croydon as London's Terminal Airport marked, therefore, the third main phase of heavier-than-air flying in Britain - from 1919 to 1929. During this time, one other aerodrome emerged, for a short period, in Surrey, now largely forgotten. It was at Byhurst Farm, Chessington, near Leatherhead.

This little aerodrome began life on 16th. February, 1920, shortly before Croydon was taken over, on the farm owned by a Mr. Pruitt. It was on the west side of Kingston Road (A243) at Malden Rushett, just South of Fairoak Lane and Chessington Zoo. The aerodrome was operated by Mr. W.G. Chapman of Leatherhead Motor Works who installed an R.E.8 hangar there, bought from Brooklands, and based a very smart D.H.6 at Chessington, an aircraft powered

Fig. 11.   Beddington and Waddon Aerodromes, with the Plough Lane buildings in 1921.

Fig. 12.   Croydon Aerodrome. The airline offices in about 1925. *[Courtesy of John Gent]*

20

Fig. 13. Croydon Airport in 1928, from the east, showing the new terminal building and hotel beside the Purley Way in the foreground and the Plough Lane buildings in process of demolition beyond.

Fig. 14. Croydon Airport, the booking hall in the Administration Building, 1928. *[Courtesy of John Gent.]*

21

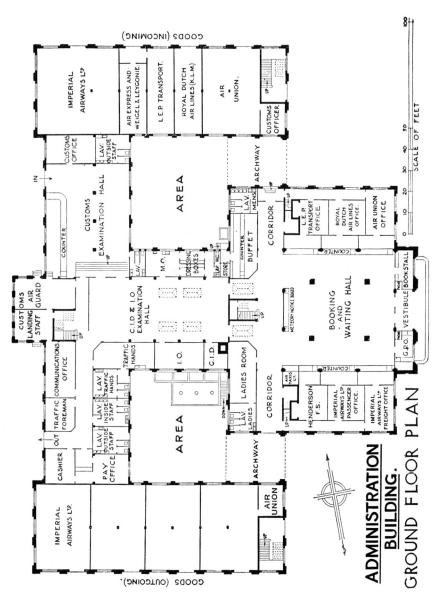

GOODS (INCOMING)

IMPERIAL AIRWAYS Lᵗᵈ

CUSTOMS OFFICE

LAV. OUTSIDE STAFF

AIR EXPRESS AND WEIGEL & LEYGONIE

L.E.P. TRANSPORT.

ROYAL DUTCH AIR LINES (K.L.M.)

AIR UNION.

CUSTOMS OFFICER

IN →

CUSTOMS EXAMINATION HALL

AREA

COUNTER

ARCHWAY

LAV. MENS

CORRIDOR

LAV.

BUFFET

COUNTER

L.E.P. TRANSPORT OFFICE

ROYAL DUTCH AIR LINES OFFICE

AIR UNION OFFICE

COUNTER

CUSTOMS LANDING AIR STAFF GUARD

TRAFFIC COMMUNICATIONS OFFICE

TRAFFIC FOREMAN

LAV.

M.O.

DRESSING BOXES

LAV. W.C.

STORE

METEOR NOTICE BOARD

BOOKING AND WAITING HALL

G.P.O.

VESTIBULE

BOOKSTALL

PHONE

C.I.D. & I.O. EXAMINATION HALL

C.I.D.

I.O.

LADIES ROOM

LAV. LADIES

CORRIDOR

AIR TAXIS Lᵗᵈ

HENDERSON F.S.

IMPERIAL AIRWAYS Lᵗˢ PASSENGER OFFICE.

IMPERIAL AIRWAYS Lᵗᵈ FREIGHT OFFICE

COUNTER

TRAFFIC HANDS

LAV. INSIDE STAFF

LAV. TRAFFIC HANDS

LAV. OUTSIDE STAFF

CASHIER

OUT

PAY OFFICE

AREA

DOWN

ARCHWAY

IMPERIAL AIRWAYS Lᵗᵈ

AIR UNION

GOODS (OUTGOING).

ADMINISTRATION BUILDING.
GROUND FLOOR PLAN

SCALE OF FEET

Fig. 15. Croydon Airport - Ground Floor Plan of the Administration Building in 1928.

22

with a 90-horse-power Curtiss OX-5 engine. This aeroplane (G-EANU) was used extensively for joy-riding and charter flights out of Chessington and became well known around the country for its smart blue colour with brass polished turn-buckles and engine cowlings. Mr. Chapman flew the D.H.6 himself and had, in addition, a professional pilot, Mr. Muir. Regrettably, on Sunday 27th. August, 1922, Chapman was seriously injured at Slough when flying as a passenger with C.A. Graham, the pilot, in an Avro 504 during an aerobatic display from which the aircraft spun in. The occupants were taken to Windsor Hospital but this spelled the end of the Leatherhead Aviation Service and the demise of Chessington as an aerodrome. The flat grass field is still to be seen.

The 'Golden Age'

So, passing through the years, we come to the second post-war phase - that is, between the Wars - from 1930 to 1939. In this 10-year period, eight aerodromes were active in Surrey, led by Croydon Airport, Brooklands and Kenley, with five new additions. The first of these was the site which was to become the second major airport of the United Kingdom and the airport handling, today, the fourth greatest number of international passengers in the World - after Heathrow, J.F.K., New York and Frankfurt. This aerodrome, first licensed to the Home Counties Aviation Services on 1st. August, 1930, but in fact used from March, 1929, was initially known as Cotland Farm Aerodrome, situated alongside the Southern Railway, just South of Gatwick Race Course, near Horley in Surrey. The detailed history of Gatwick Airport has been told in a book published by the Gatwick Branch of the Royal Aeronautical Society, written by John King and Geoff. Tate, and I need do no more than sketch in the outline here. I, myself, landed at Gatwick for the first time just 53 years ago, on 6th. November, 1932, having flown down from Cambridge by way of Croydon to have tea and crumpets in the delightful little Elizabethan cottage which served as a club house. In those days, Gatwick was run by the Surrey Aero Club which owned a D.H. Moth and a Robinson Redwing biplane and it was, in fact, acquired by Redwing Aircraft Limited from Croydon, a year later. Then, in October 1934, Airports Limited was formed to acquire Gatwick and, on 6th. June, 1936, Lord Swinton, the Secretary of State for Air, opened Gatwick as a grass airport with the Martello Tower - or 'Beehive' - terminal building, connected to a Gatwick railway station by means of a subway. In those days, the landing area was 1,000 yards by 700 yards. Though bedevilled with waterlogged conditions during winter months, as a result of flooding from the River Mole - which caused British Airways to move out of Gatwick to Heston in May of 1938 - Gatwick gradually built up as a commercial airport as an alternate to Croydon up to the start of the Second World War.

By this time, four other aerodromes were active in Surrey. The first of these was at Addington, three miles south east of Croydon, where the British Air Transport Company, which had taken over the Henderson School of Flying at Croydon and Brooklands, moved in with four Gipsy Moths, one Fox Moth, one Puss Moth, one Miles Hawk and one C.30 Cierva autogyro. Addington was, however, too small to be satisfactory for all-the-year-round flying and B.A.T. moved from Addington to Gatwick in 1933 and then on to Redhill, (of which more in a moment) in November, 1934.

Fig. 16.   Cotland Farm Airfield, Gatwick, with Hunts Green Farm, 1932.

Fig. 17.   The Opening of Gatwick Aerodrome, 6th. June, 1936.

24

Fig. 18. Gatwick Aerodrome. The Beehive is nearly complete in this 1936 photograph, which also shows the British Airways Hangar in the foreground. To the right is the track of the London/Brighton railway and the new Railway Station. *[Courtesy of John King]*.

Fig. 19. Gatwick Aerodrome. The Beehive and the new Railway Station in 1936.

25

Fig. 20. A Fokker F.XII of British Airways Ltd., outside the Beehive at Gatwick. Note the telescopic passageways from the Terminal to the Aircraft. *[Courtesy of John King.]*

In the meantime, another small aerodrome had been laid out at Ditton Hill, Hook, alongside the Kingston Bypass. It was licensed in June of 1933, one-and-a-half miles south of Surbiton, with a landing area 400 yards by 270 yards and adjoining the Southboro' Arms Hotel. One of its attractions was, also, the neighbouring 'Ace of Spades' garage, restaurant and swimming pool. Hook Aerodrome flourished for three years until its restrictive size proved too difficult even for the aircraft of those days and, today, it is covered with small houses.

The brief lives of Addington and Hook were followed in May of 1934 by the acquisition by B.A.T. of a hundred-acre site to the south east of Redhill near Nutfield. B.A.T. moved into what was to become Redhill Aerodrome in November, 1934, a field in which a dominant feature was, as at Brooklands, a large sewage farm, the location of which meant that aircraft had to taxi down a lane, through a gateway, to reach the flying field. In March, 1935, B.A.T. gained a contract for training Imperial Airways engineers for 'B' licences and for basic flying training and on Saturday, 13th. April, 1935, Sir Alan Cobham selected Redhill for the opening of his 1935 National Aviation Day tour. A crowd of more than 3,000 people watched the show which included spectacular aerobatics from Geoffrey Tyson, flying an Avro Tutor, and parachute descents from the one and only Handley Page Clive. Redhill Flying Club was formed in March, 1937, to take part in the Civil Air Guard scheme, and, in July, 1937, No.15 Elementary and Reserve Flying Training School, R.A.F., opened at Redhill equipped with, at first, Gipsy Moths, and then Tiger Moths, then Magisters and, eventually, from October, 1937, two Hawker Hart trainers as well. Six new hangars were built at Redhill in 1938, by which time Redhill had

26

Fig. 21. **Redhill Aerodrome,** under construction in 1934. *[Courtesy of John King]*

Fig. 22. **Redhill Aerodrome in 1982.**

14 Magisters, 14 Hart trainers and six Fairey Battles, with nine instructors and 115 pupils under training. By then, the Nutfield Sewage Farm had been acquired and incorporated into the aerodrome and three Avro Ansons were added to the strength. Just before the War, on 29th. July, 1939, a major air display was held at Redhill and, remarkably, aircraft which landed and gave demonstrations included, from Imperial Airways an Armstrong-Whitworth Ensign, from British Airways a Lockheed 14, from Sabena a DC-3 and from Luft Hansa a Focke-Wolf Condor, as well as, from the Royal Air Force, a Hawker Hurricane and a Vickers Wellington bomber.

The list of Surrey's between-the-Wars aerodromes was completed in 1935 by the setting-up of a small private aerodrome at Warlingham by Charles Gardner, who owned a variety of private aircraft, including a Mew Gull. Like Addington and Hook, Warlingham, three-and-a-half miles South East of Croydon, had a short existence - up to 1939. But it deserves to be remembered as a delightful private aerodrome in those pre-war days of relatively uninhibited private aviation.

During all this time, Brooklands had prospered with a strong Brooklands Flying Club and Flying School and active aircraft manufacture on the part of the new Hawker Siddeley Group and Vickers. Modern hangars had been put up in the south-west corner of the aerodrome to replace the remains of the original 1910 buildings. From them came the first of the great series of Hawker Hart and Fury day-bomber and interceptor aircraft and, alongside, from the Vickers Works the Vildebeests, to be succeeded by the Wellesley and then the Wellington, bombers.

Hawker Aircraft Limited had, in 1935, become part of the new Hawker Siddeley Aircraft Company with its headquarters at Kingston. Its fortunes were founded on the success of the large-scale production of Hawker Hart variants. Indeed more than 2,800 Harts and their variants, such as the Hind, the Audax, the Demon, the Hector and the Hardy, were built in the late 1930s for the Royal Air Force, the Royal Navy and for 20 other air forces. Thus, the Hart was the first British aircraft to be exported in substantial numbers, founding not only the fortunes of Hawker Aircraft Limited but also those of Rolls Royce Limited, with its Kestrel aero engine, selected also as the power plant for the Hawker Fury single-seat, interceptor fighter, built at Kingston and flown from Brooklands. More than 350 Hawker Fury biplane fighters went into service - one of the most delightful aeroplanes of its day and the first in the Royal Air Force to exceed 200 miles an hour.

Then came the end of the biplane era and the rebirth of the monoplane, now with stressed-skin construction, retractable undercarriages, variable-pitch propellers and a significant advance in performance in all respects. The Hurricane, with its Rolls-Royce Merlin engine, set a new standard in fighter performance. It had a top speed of 315 miles an hour, allied to delightful handling qualities. The first production Hurricane was flown from Brooklands on 12th. October, 1937, and by September, 1939, 18 Hurricane squadrons were in service with Royal Air Force Fighter Command. In all, more than 14,200 Hurricanes were built in the United Kingdom and Canada.

Alongside the Hawker Aircraft Company at Brooklands, Vickers-Armstrongs Limited concentrated on the production of larger aircraft - most significantly the Vickers Wellington bomber, the first of which, with its geodetic construction, originated by Barnes Wallis, made its first flight at Brooklands on 15th. June,

Fig. 23. Brooklands School of Flying, in the 1930s, showing the new Control Tower and Clubhouse of 1932. *[Courtesy of Brooklands Museum.]*

Fig. 24. Brooklands, 1939. *[Courtesy of Brooklands Museum.]*

MISS AMY JOHNSON. O.B.E.

Fig. 25. Miss Amy Johnson returned to Croydon Aerodrome on August Bank Holiday 1930. *[Courtesy of John Gent]*

1936, piloted by Mutt Summers, to be followed by the first production Wellington on 23rd. December, 1937 - the first of 11,461 to be built - 2,451 of them at Brooklands.

Meanwhile, Croydon was moving with the times. In October, 1934, the MacRobertson Air Race was run from Mildenhall to Melbourne, Australia, won by Charles Scott and Tom Campbell-Black in the D.H. Comet Racer. The aircraft which came in second was K.L.M.'s first Douglas DC-2 carrying 11 passengers, the first of the new generation of low-wing, twin-engined aircraft with retractable undercarriage and all-metal construction and first seen at Croydon early in October 1934. In place of the H.P.42s, there came also a new generation of four-motor, low-wing monoplanes for Imperial Airways. One of the first of them, the de Havilland D.H. 91 Albatross of the Frobisher Class set up scheduled times of less than one hour between Croydon and Le Bourget. In the summer of 1939, Croydon had never been busier. Although the flying-boats had taken over the main long-distance Empire air routes to Australia and to South Africa, as well as on experimental services across the North Atlantic; European air traffic had started to grow substantially and air transport was becoming a normal means of Continental travel. On the eve of war, Croydon turned over from an international civil airport to become a fighter station. It was to suffer grievous bombing during the Battle of Britain. So we come to the end of an era with the start of the Second World War.

Fig. 26. Kenley Airfield in 1937.

31

Second World War

Yet again, Brooklands was placed on a military footing and both the Hawkers and Vickers Companies concentrated on aircraft production and development flying from Brooklands. The prototype Hawker Tornado, to replace the Hurricane, was flown from Brooklands in October, 1939, to be followed by the prototype Typhoon on 24th. February, 1940. In 1942, however, the Hawker Aircraft Company acquired a new aerodrome at Langley, in Buckinghamshire, near Heathrow, to cope with their increasing production and test flying. Brooklands concentrated on the development and production flying of the increasing numbers of Vickers aircraft.

Fig. 27. Fairoaks in 1942, from a mosaic of vertical air photographs.

Almost six years of War, between 1939 and 1945, brought with it a near elimination of civil flying in Britain. But it brought, at the same time, a vast increase in military aviation. The result was, not only increased activity at Brooklands, as a base for aircraft manufacture, and the elevation of Kenley into the front line as a fighter station during the Battle of Britain and subsequently, but, also, the switch of Croydon, Gatwick and Redhill from civil aviation to become Royal Air Force fighter bases. With all of this, seven new aerodromes were added to the remaining five in Surrey. The new Fields, in order of initiation, were Fairoaks, Lingfield, Egham, Dunsfold, Hurst Park, Wisley and Horne, while Brooklands, Kenley, Croydon, Gatwick and Redhill all continued under Royal Air Force aegis. Of the others, Hook, Addington and Warlingham disappeared from the aviation scene.

After the War

With the end of the War, Dunsfold was the reception centre for prisoner-of-war repatriation and large numbers of Douglas Dakota aircraft and Handley Page Halifaxes, converted for troop carrying, landed at Dunsfold, carrying British, American and Canadian prisoners back to the United Kingdom. Dunsfold was acquired by Skyways Limited as its chief maintenance base under Ronald Ashley, flying Avro Yorks and Douglas DC-4s from its hard runway. Dunsfold was acquired by the Hawker Siddeley Group in 1952 and first used by Hawker Aircraft for development work on Hawker Hunter jet fighters, the first of which was flown at Boscombe Down in July, 1951. During the next few years, Dunsfold was a centre of Hunter production and development flying, while assembly shops and experimental flight amenities were set up alongside the runway. Of great future significance, hovering trials of the vertical take-off Hawker P.1127 prototype - the forerunner of the Hawker Harrier - began at Dunsfold on 21st. October, 1960, flown by Bill Bedford - followed by untethered, hovering flights on 19th. November, 1960. Thereafter, Harrier development work and production test flying went forward at Dunsfold - and continues to this day. Dunsfold has, therefore, taken over from Brooklands and from Langley as a major centre of fighter development and production test flying.

Fig. 28. Dunsfold Aerodrome in 1979.

Meanwhile, at Wisley, two-and-a-half miles south west of Brooklands, Captain Mutt Summers (for many years Chief Test Pilot of Vickers Armstrongs) had force-landed a Vickers Wellesley in a large, smooth field just before the

33

War. When a new aerodrome was required to supplement Brooklands for Vickers test flying, Mutt Summers remembered this forced landing of his and the Wisley site was surveyed. By the clearing of a few hedges and trees, an unobstructed grass runway, of some 2,300 yards, was laid out, with good approaches. Work began on the site in 1943 and, eventually, in 1952, a runway 6,700 feet long by 220 feet wide was laid with night landing facilities. By 1944, Wisley was in full operation with new flight sheds to house a series of experimental aircraft. New buildings and offices were added after the War. A great series of post-war aircraft made their first flights at Wisley. The first of these was the Vickers Viking, which went into service with B.E.A. One of the prototypes was converted to Nene jet engines and contributed some valuable development flying, leading to the new civil jet transport era. In 1949, the prototype Viscount V.630 was flown from Wisley - the first of the most successful post-War British turbine-powered transport aircraft, of which more than 400 were built. On 29th. July, 1950, the prototype Viscount inaugurated the World's first scheduled turbine-powered commercial air service from Northolt to Le Bourget. Viscounts went into regular service with B.E.A. in 1952, a happy collaboration between the designers and manufacturers, Vickers Limited, led by George Edwards, and B.E.A., of which I was then Chief Executive. Wisley remained in the forefront of development flying during the 1950s and the 1960s, including the first flights of the Varsity, Valetta and the Valient jet bomber. Meanwhile Vickers Vanguard, the VC-10 and the Super VC-10 all made their first flights from a new hard runway at Brooklands but they made their first landings at Wisley and all the B.A.C. civil aircraft which followed the Viscount did most of their development flying from Wisley, including the B.A.C. One-Eleven. The final flight out of Wisley was made on 28th. May, 1972, by the B.A.C.-owned de Havilland Heron (G-ANNO), flown by Brian Trubshaw.

Meanwhile, the hard runway had been laid down at Brooklands in 1948, cutting the Byfleet banking of the former motor race track. By now, Brooklands was the centre of the newly-formed British Aircraft Corporation, under Sir George Edwards. But, a little earlier than this in June, 1954, there was a nostalgic return to Brooklands of its very first aeronautical inhabitant. A plaque was unveiled near the site of A. V. Roe's original shops of 1908 and a presentation made to Sir Alliot Verdon-Roe by Tom Gammon, General Manager of Vickers Armstrongs Limited. Brooklands remained as a test centre for a few more years and the last aircraft to be designed and constructed wholly at Brooklands was the Super VC-10.

The Present Phase

And so we come to the final phase of this 200-year history of aeronautics and aviation in Surrey. During the past few years, there have been further major advances in technology as both military and civil aircraft have moved up to - and now substantially beyond - Mach 1, the speed of sound, and as air transport has grown to be the chief means of international passenger travel. As the skies have become more crowded and the major airports more congested, so private flying has become more difficult and more expensive. The business helicopter is, however, now in service in increasing numbers and there are about a dozen

Fig. 29.   Wisley Airfield, from over Ockham in September 1968.

helicopter sites in Surrey licensed for every-day take-offs and landings. On the manufacturing side, the building, the development and the flying of new aircraft have become much more complex and much more costly. A result has been a concentration of aerodromes into a few major sites. And the past few years have seen the disappearance from the active flying scene of many of the historic centres.

The most historic of these casualties has been Brooklands although it remained the headquarters of the Aircraft Division of British Aerospace. From an aviation point of view, the great days of flying at Brooklands were between 1910 and 1914 and between 1925 and 1939, followed by its role as a major manufacturing base for Vickers Armstrongs during the Second World War. Then Brooklands was the birthplace of the outstanding series of Vickers aircraft which followed the Wellington Bomber up to the Super VC-10. Appropriately enough, the last business flights outbound from Brooklands and in-bound into Brooklands were both flown by Sir George Edwards, at that time Chairman of the British Aircraft Corporation (B.A.C.). On 30th. June, 1975, Sir George took off in the B.A.C. Beagle B.206 (G-AVHO), flying from Brooklands to Warton, returning the following day, 1st. July, 1975, from Salmesbury. Thus ended - after 65 years and seven months the long and distinguished history of Brooklands as a British flying centre - from Louis Paulhan's first take-off on 29th. October, 1909, to Sir George Edwards' last landing there on 1st. July, 1975. A final and informal stage was when on the fiftieth anniversary of the first flight of the Hawker Hurricane prototype, Squadron Leader John Ward, of the Battle of Britain Flight of the Royal Air Force, flew in to Brooklands the very

35

Fig. 30. Brooklands, from the south east in 1960, showing the runway made in 1948.

Fig. 31. Brooklands, the B.A.C. Works from the east in May 1973.

Fig. 32. **Gatwick Airport,** from the east in 1984.

last production Hurricane, 'The Last of the Many'. Wing Commander John Ward flew out again on 7th. November, 1985, and so completed that story. Only Farnborough, in Hampshire, and Shoreham, in Sussex, can now boast a longer association with British fixed-wing flying.

Now also, Kenley has gone - it remains a field of waving grasses, haunted by the whispering echoes of rotary engines, or early Sopwith Pups and Camels and the mellow tones of later Rolls-Royce Merlins in Hurricanes and Spitfires. Croydon, too, has gone, its last flight, out-bound - appropriately by Captain Geoffrey Last, flying a D.H. Heron - on 29th. September, 1959. And Wisley, too, has returned to its former rural state.

In 1985, more than 14 million passengers will have passed through Gatwick - and its growth continues, though severely hampered by the short-sighted restriction of the Airport to a single main runway. Gatwick is now, indeed, by a long way the busiest airport in the World confined to one runway. And as an active memory of its early days as an airport - 50 years ago next year - the 'Beehive' still thrives. And deep in the Surrey countryside, Dunsfold remains, seven miles from Guildford - a great aircraft test-centre on the forefront of military VTOL development.

Fig. 33. **The Brooklands Clubhouse today,** now restored to be the central feature of the Spirit of Brooklands Museum of British Motorsport and Aviation. The first-floor room on the left, with the verandah, was Sir Barnes Wallis's Office. [*Courtesy of Brooklands Museum*].

So, 200 years have come and gone and, with them, the most remarkable change in Man's ability to cover time and space. Surrey has, indeed, played an important part in this long trail of human progress. So let us end where we began the story of fixed-wing aviation - back at Brooklands. The sound of Merlin, Dart, Spey and Conway engines at Brooklands has now ceased but it remains a thriving centre of high technology and of employment in British aviation as the headquarters of British Aerospace's Aircraft Division. Out of all the 45 sites which have been the basis of so much endeavour, only five now remain, in addition to the Weybridge base. Flying continues at Gatwick, Dunsfold, Redhill, Fairoaks and the private aerodrome at Ridinghurst Farm at Cranleigh. Between them, they represent the whole spectrum of aviation at the end of the 20th. century - from helicopters to VTOL military aircraft, from light, fixed-wing, aircraft to the 500-passenger commercial jets, taking off daily from Gatwick to fly, non-stop, in one direction to Hong Kong and in the other to Los Angeles. One can do no more than contemplate what the next 200 years may bring. I suspect no less great developments are awaiting our great-grandchildren than any of those from the days of the fragile balloons of 1785 to the supersonic aircraft of today.

[Since Sir Peter Masefield gave his talk we have seen the demise of several famous factories from Surrey. British Aerospace have left Brooklands, the historic parts of which have now opened as a museum of motorsport and aviation, and the old Hawker building in Kingston has become part of Kingston University, while demolition has commenced on their later factory in Richmond Road. Also there has been another 'last landing' at Brooklands in 1987, when a VC-10 arrived from Oman.]

SURREY
AERODROMES

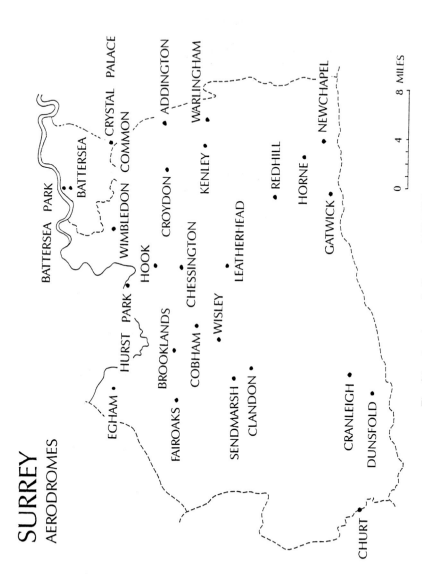

Fig. 34. Aerodromes in Surrey - 1907/1986.

THE ELEVEN HISTORIC SITES OF LIGHTER-THAN-AIR FLYING IN SURREY

1785 TO 1920.

Location	Aeronauts	First Flight
Hurst Park, Molesey	James Sadler, William Windham	1 May 1785
St. George's Fields, Southwark	Mrs. Sage, Colonel Biggin	29 June 1785
The Ranelagh Club, Barn Elms	A.G. Ganerin, Capt. R.C. Sowden	28 June 1802
Vauxhall Gardens, Kennington	A.G. Ganerin	3 August 1802
Surrey Zoological Gardens, Walworth	J.W. Hoare	24 May 1838
Phoenix Gas Works, Kennington	Hugh Bells	8 May 1850
The Crystal Palace, Upper Norwood	Henry Coxwell, James Glaisher	August 1859
Battersea Gas Works, South Lambeth	Short Brothers	September 1903
Wandsworth Gas Works, Wandsworth	J.L. Tanner	7 April 1906
The Polo Ground, The Roehampton Club, Roehampton		August 1914
Mitcham Gas Works, Mitcham	A. Newall	26 February 1920

AIRSHIPS IN SURREY

1902 TO 1910

1. From Crystal Palace, Upper Norwood to Eastcote   22 September 1902
    Stanley Spencer
    22 Miles in 1 hour 40 minutes
    The First Powered Flight by an Airship in England

2. To Crystal Palace from Aldershot   5 October 1907
    British Army Airship No. 1. 'Nulli Secundus'
    J.E. Capper and S.F. Cody
    50 Miles in 3 hours 25 minutes

3. To Crystal Palace from Cardiff *via* Lee, Kent   6/8 August 1910
    Willows Airship No. 2.
    E.T. Willows
    150 Miles in two days

4. To Redhill from Farnborough, Hampshire   1 July 1913
    H.M. Airship 'Delta'

5. To Gatton Park, Reigate from Farnborough   November 1914
    H.M. Airship 'Eta'

FOUR BASES OF AIRCRAFT MANUFACTURE & ASSEMBLY IN SURREY

BROOKLANDS *Avro, Bleriot, Glenny & Henderson, Hawker, Martinsyde, Sopwith, Vickers, B.A.C. and British Aerospace.*

CROYDON *National Aircraft Factory No. 1., A.D.C., Desoutter and General Aircraft.*

DUNSFOLD *Hawker, B.A.C. and British Aerospace.*

WISLEY *Vickers and B.A.C.*

SURREY FLYING SERVICES,
LIMITED.
CROYDON AERODROME.
Britain's Oldest Flying School.

Telephone : Croydon 1736.   'Grams : " Aviation, 'Phone, Croydon."

PLEASURE FLIGHTS.
3 SEATER AVRO MACHINES (Open seaters)
The World's Acknowledged Safest Aircraft.

Half a Million Passengers have been carried on this type of Aeroplane, by Surrey Flying Services, Ltd., without accident to Passengers.

FLIGHTS **5/-**   CHILDREN **2/6d.**
per passenger.

SALOON MACHINES.
1931 PUSS MOTHS.
The Real Luxury Aeroplane.

FLIGHTS from **5/-** per passenger.

Flights over London in these machines £1-1-0 per passenger.

FLYING SCHOOL.
Tuition on Moth Aeroplanes £3 per hour Dual and £3-10-0 per hour Solo Flying.   TRIAL LESSON £1-1-0.   Special Terms for A and B complete licences.   **NIGHT FLYING INSTRUCTION.**

Be sure you Fly with
SURREY FLYING SERVICES, LTD.
Who have been Operating at Croydon Aerodrome for 11 Years.

SAFETY FIRST.

Fig. 35. An Advertisement from the 1932 Air Ministry Guidebook to the 'Airport of London (Croydon)'.